COLDPLAY

PIANO
VOCAL
GUITAR

ISBN 978-1-4584-2223-1

HAL•LEONARD®
CORPORATION
7777 W. BLUEMOUND RD. P.O. BOX 13819 MILWAUKEE, WI 53213

Visit Hal Leonard Online at
www.halleonard.com

COLDPLAY

MYLO XYLOTO

The guitar chord boxes in this book are shown in conventional tuning (EADGBE).
This table shows the guitar tunings supplied by Chris Martin
to show how Coldplay perform these songs:

HURTS LIKE HEAVEN
EBEG#BE (CAPO 6)

CHARLIE BROWN
EADGAD (CAPO 4)

US AGAINST THE WORLD
EADF#AE (CAPO 3)

EVERY TEARDROP IS A WATERFALL
DADGAE

MAJOR MINUS
EADGBE (CAPO 10)

PRINCESS OF CHINA
EADGBE (CAPO 10)

U.F.O.
CGDGBD (CAPO 2)

UP WITH THE BIRDS
EADGBD (CAPO 7)

MYLO XYLOTO

Words and Music by GUY BERRYMAN,
JON BUCKLAND, WILL CHAMPION,
CHRIS MARTIN and BRIAN ENO

HURTS LIKE HEAVEN

Words and Music by GUY BERRYMAN,
JON BUCKLAND, WILL CHAMPION,
CHRIS MARTIN and BRIAN ENO

you_____ use your heart as a weap-on._____ And it hurts_____ like heav-en._____

(Guitar solo ad lib. on D.S.)

PARADISE

Words and Music by GUY BERRYMAN,
JON BUCKLAND, WILL CHAMPION,
CHRIS MARTIN and BRIAN ENO

1. When she was just a girl, she ex-pec-ted the world. But it

flew a-way from her reach. So she ran a-way in her sleep and dreamed of

CHARLIE BROWN

Words and Music by GUY BERRYMAN,
JON BUCKLAND, WILL CHAMPION,
CHRIS MARTIN and BRIAN ENO

Gm
E♭
B♭
3fr
6fr
1. Stole a key. Took a
Gm
E♭
Cm7
car down town where the lost boys meet. Took a car down town and took what they of - fered me
Gm
E♭
B♭
to set me free. I saw the
Gm
E♭
Cm7
lights go down at the end of the scene. I saw the lights go down and stand-ing in front of me.

US AGAINST THE WORLD

Words and Music by GUY BERRYMAN,
JON BUCKLAND, WILL CHAMPION,
CHRIS MARTIN and BRIAN ENO

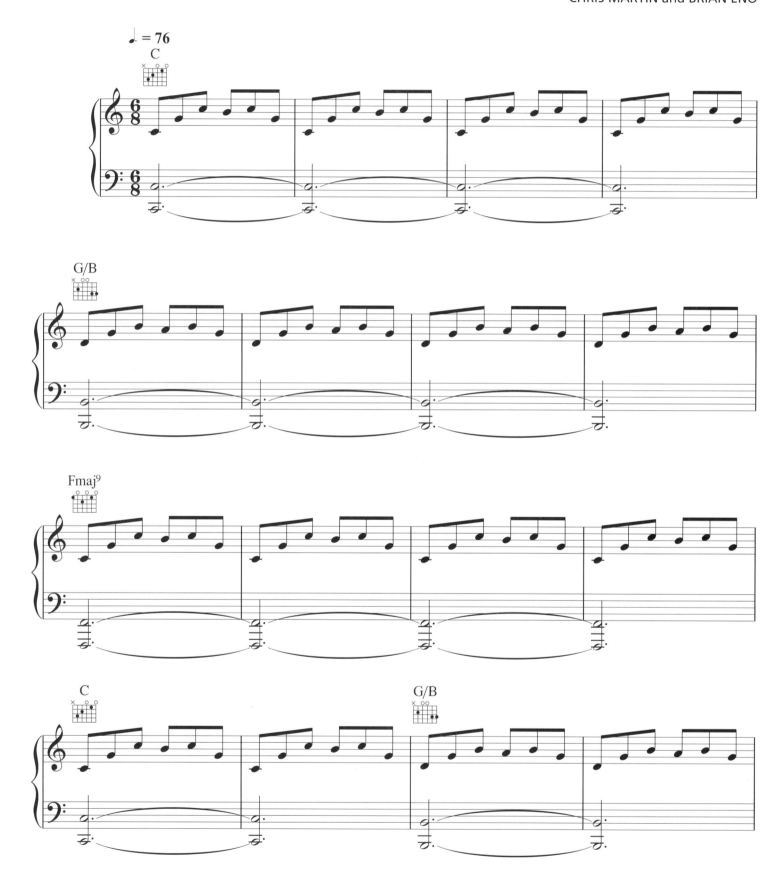

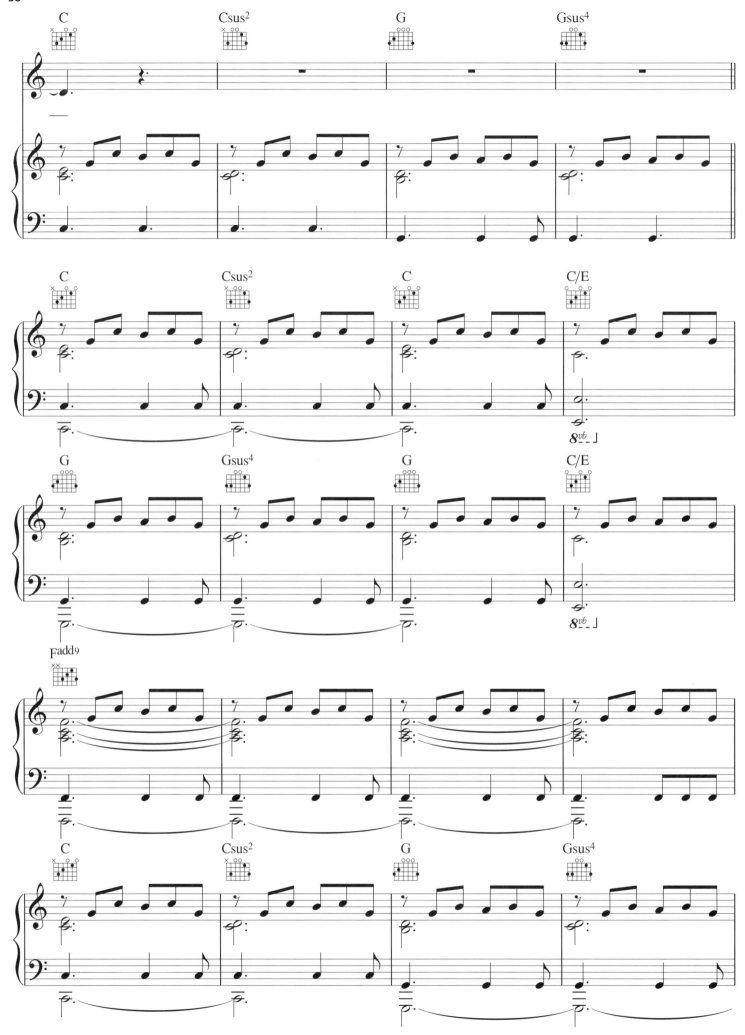

M.M.I.X.

Words and Music by GUY BERRYMAN,
JON BUCKLAND, WILL CHAMPION,
CHRIS MARTIN and BRIAN ENO

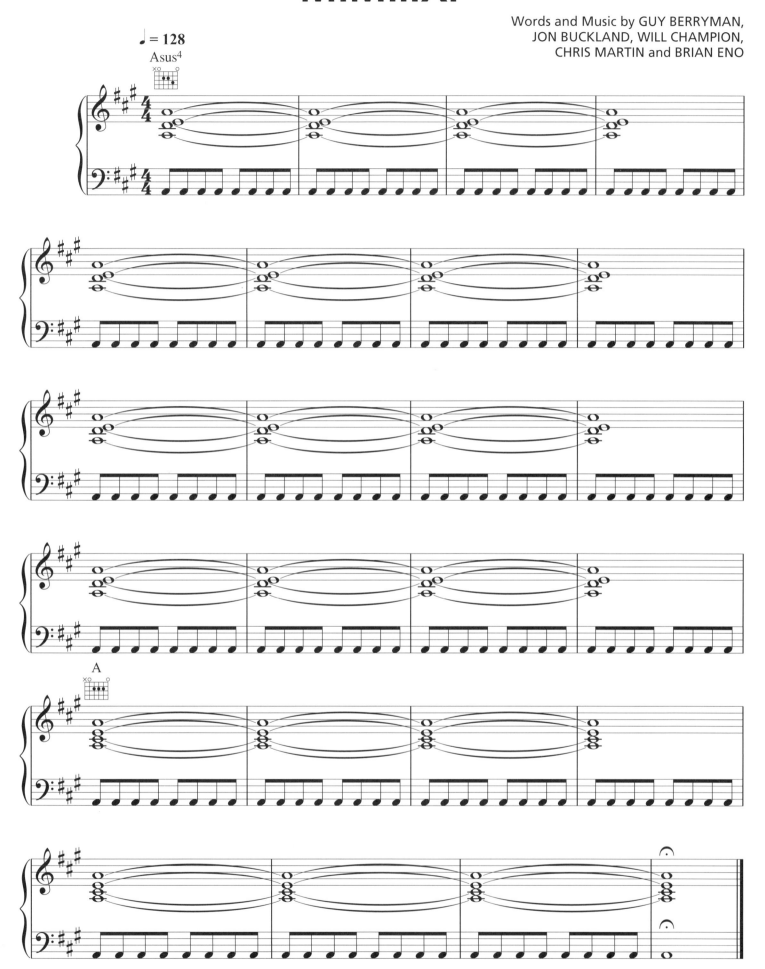

EVERY TEARDROP IS A WATERFALL

Words and Music by GUY BERRYMAN,
JON BUCKLAND, WILL CHAMPION,
CHRIS MARTIN, PETER ALLEN,
ADRIENNE ANDERSON and BRIAN ENO

MAJOR MINUS

Words and Music by GUY BERRYMAN,
JON BUCKLAND, WILL CHAMPION,
CHRIS MARTIN and BRIAN ENO

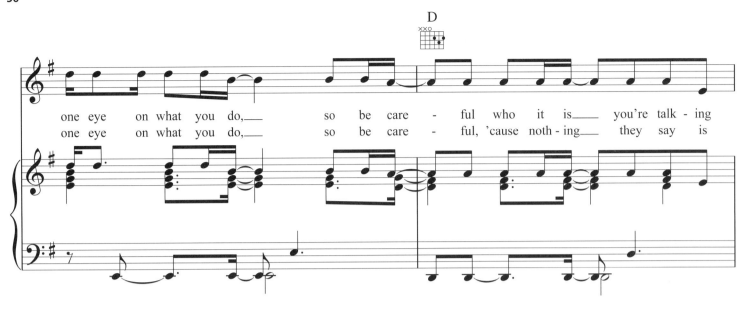

one eye on what you do,___ so be care - ful who it is___ you're talk - ing
one eye on what you do,___ so be care - ful, 'cause noth - ing___ they say is

to. They got one eye watch - ing you,___
true. But then___ don't be - lieve a word;___ it's just

one eye on what you do,___ so be care - ful what it is___ you're try'n' to do;
us a - gainst the world, and we_____ just got - ta turn__ up to be heard.

Got one eye on the road and one on...
one eye on the road and one on...
(She can

hear them climb-ing the stairs. I got my right side fight-ing while my left hides un-der chairs.)

con ped.

senza ped.

E⁷

Guitar solo

B⁷

E⁷

B⁷

1.

2.

Ooh, ooh._____ Ooh, ooh._____ Got

one eye on the road__ and one on you.__ Ooh, ooh._____ Ooh, ooh._____

____ Got one eye on the road__ and one on you.

U.F.O.

Words and Music by GUY BERRYMAN,
JON BUCKLAND, WILL CHAMPION,
CHRIS MARTIN and BRIAN ENO

PRINCESS OF CHINA

Words and Music by GUY BERRYMAN,
JON BUCKLAND, WILL CHAMPION,
CHRIS MARTIN, JON BIRGISSON,
ORRI DYRASON, GEORG HOLM,
KJARTEN SVEINSSON and BRIAN ENO

Once up-on a time we fell a-part. You're hold-ing in your hands the two___ halves of my heart.

Oh.___ Oh.___

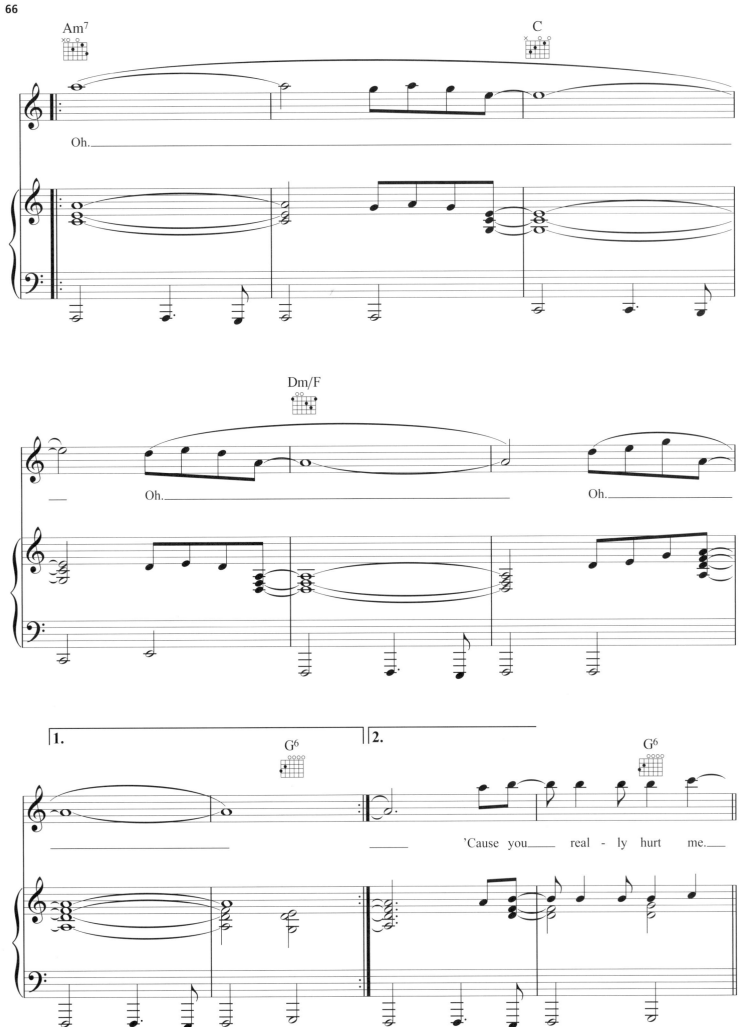

UP IN FLAMES

Words and Music by GUY BERRYMAN,
JON BUCKLAND, WILL CHAMPION,
and CHRIS MARTIN

♩ = 76

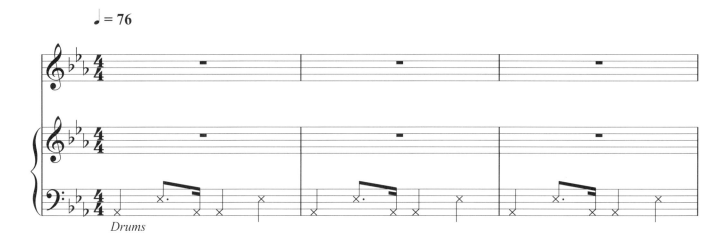

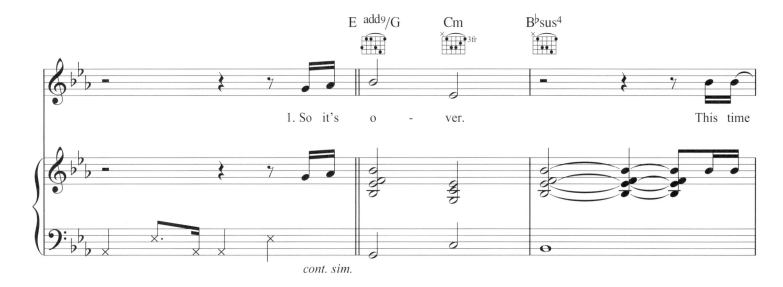

1. So it's o - ver. This time

cont. sim.

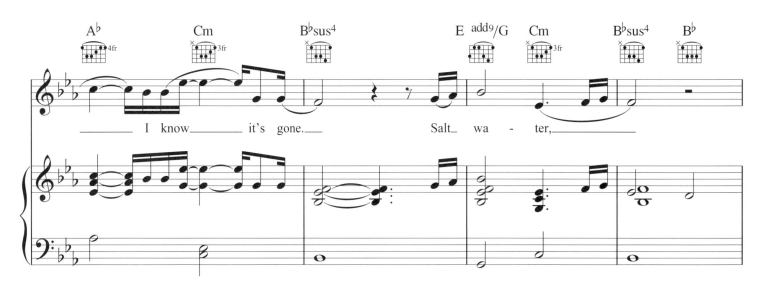

I know it's gone. Salt wa - ter,

A HOPEFUL TRANSMISSION

Words and Music by GUY BERRYMAN,
JON BUCKLAND, WILL CHAMPION,
CHRIS MARTIN and BRIAN ENO

DON'T LET IT BREAK YOUR HEART

Words and Music by GUY BERRYMAN,
JON BUCKLAND, WILL CHAMPION,
and CHRIS MARTIN

1. And ... if I___ lost the

find you nev - er left___ the start.

Come on___ ba - by, don't let it___ break your

heart."

Though

heav - i - ly we

78

Don't let it____ break your heart. *(echo)*

UP WITH THE BIRDS

Words and Music by GUY BERRYMAN,
JON BUCKLAND, WILL CHAMPION,
CHRIS MARTIN, BRIAN ENO
and LEONARD COHEN

up_____ to that won - der - ful world._____

And then_____ I'm up with_____ the birds.

♩ = 120 a tempo

A sim-ple plot,___ Oh,___ yeah!___

Con pedale